"Seeking-Arms" CHUM-KIU

Published worldwide in English, Chinese, German, French, Spanish, Hungarian, Italian and other languages.

WRITTEN BY
GRANDMASTER PROFESSOR LEUNG TING
Golden Rank Founder of the International WingTsun Association,
Ph D in Philosophy, Guest Professor of the National Sport Academy in Bulgaria

Chief Demonstrator:
GREAT MASTER CHENG CHUEN FUN
9th Level M.O.A., IWTA

ISBN: 962-7284-75-0
First Edition: 1 Dec 2002
Second Edition: 1 May 2003
Third Edition: 1 Jan 2007
Fourth Edition: 18 Nov 2011

Chief Editor
LEUNG WAI BUN

English Translating
JANE ZHEN

Proof Reading
SIFU KEITH SONNENBERG
(4th Level Technician, IWTA)

Copyright © 2002 November by Leung's Publications, Hong Kong
Flat 4C, Chak Fung Building, 440-442 Nathan Road, Kowloon, Hong Kong
Fax: (852) 2780-8181 \ 2771-2048 \ E-mail: iwtahk@gmail.com

leungting.com \ iwta.com

Contents

About the Founder of the IWTA
Grandmaster Professor Leung Ting

*P*rofessor Leung Ting, the IWTA founder and the only "Golden Rank" (Founder's Level) holder of the International WingTsun Association, the Honorary Chief Instructor of the Hungarian Police Karate Section and the Guest Chief-Instructor of Indian National Police Academy, is also a recognized scholar with a Bachelor of Arts in Chinese and English Literature and a Doctor of Philosophy in Philosophy. In addition to these achievements, he was honored with the title "Guest Professor of Combat Arts" by the National Sport of Bulgaria in 1997.

Leung Ting began studying Wing Chun at the age of 13. When he was at 17, he assisted his marital uncle Cheng Buck (鄭北), who was also a *Si-Hing* (師兄 — *senior kungfu fellow-student or "elder kungfu brother" as in kungfu terminology*) of Leung, to teach Wing Chun kungfu in a rough tin-rooftop school. After graduation from high school, Leung was enrolled in the Baptist College. He was soon convinced by his *Si-Dais* (師弟— *younger kungfu brothers*) *to* begin teaching them Wing Chun as a part-time job in the evening.

In 1968, Sifu Leung opened a WingTsun class in the Baptist College; the first Chinese kungfu class ever being run in a post-secondary institute in Hong Kong.

During that time the late Great Grandmaster Yip Man had just *"closed his door"* (*retired from teaching*). However, he accepted Leung Ting as his personal student and gave him private tutorials in the most advanced techniques and theories of Wing Tsun.

Left: A photo taken in summer 1969, when the late Great Grandmaster Yip Man was teaching Wooden Dummy Techniques to Sifu Leung Ting in Leung's Second *Si-Hing* Kwok Keung's home.

After finding out the differences between what he had learned from his first instructor and Great Grandmaster Yip Man during the very last period of the Great Grandmaster's life, he soon registered the title of his own kungfu system as "Wing Tsun"; hence "Wing Tsun" became the special term of the International organizations of the Leung Ting kungfu system identified from the generic term "Wing Chun" or "Ving Tsun" used by the other students of Grandmaster Yip Man. *(WingTsun™ is later spelled as one word, internationally.)*

Since his graduation from the Hong Kong Baptist College in 1973, Sifu Leung Ting devoted all his energy in developing WingTsun kungfu. At present, the International WingTsun Association has grown into a worldwide kungfu organization with branches in over 63 countries and is regarded as the largest professional kungfu organization in the world. This growth is a tribute to Professor Leung Ting's endless and indomitable effort.

The miraculous speed of development of WingTsun kungfu to the other martial artists is so far not that satisfying to Professor Leung Ting! He has never slowed down in his intensive study on the subject of WingTsun kungfu and the methods of teaching kungfu in the decades since his first lessons. Besides the successive refinement on the traditional WingTsun system in recent years, to meet the demand of the military guard of various countries, Professor Leung worked out the most practical WT ways to teach different sets of techniques in overcoming the enemy in a few seconds under any circumstances. Today, Professor Leung's WingTsun is practiced world-wide by hundreds of thousands of martial-art instructors of special forces, such as the FBI of the USA, SEK of Germany, RAID of France, NOCS of Italy, GIP of Luxembourg, and special police units of Spain, Belgium, Austria, India and Hungary, etc. And even instructors from the special police unit of the Community of Independent States (CIS) and air-borne special force of Egypt apply WingTsun combat techniques. Especially in Europe, over 70% of the special forces either adopt Prof Leung Ting's WingTsun kungfu or at least combine some WingTsun techniques in their bare-hand fighting courses.

Many WingTsun practitioners, before they become members of the International WingTsun Association, are already martial-art experts in different styles and have already obtained titles of national champions, runner-ups, and even world-champions in different martial-art tournaments. Therefore, even as early as the end of the 60's, Sifu Leung Ting was being referred to as the *"Kungfu Instructor of Millions of Students"* by the media in Hong Kong. The fighters he trained had brilliant results in full contact matches so he was entitled the *"Trainer of Fighters"* by the magazines. In recent decades, he was also referred to as the *"WingTsun King"* and *"Genghis Khan in the Kungfu Circle".*

Apart from developing WingTsun kungfu, Professor Leung has written, published and produced quite a few books and videotapes on various kungfu styles. Between the mid 70's and 80's, he was once engaged in TV broadcasting and film productions as a technical director and planner for the 24-episode TV series *"Real*

Kungfu" for the Rediffusion Television Station of HK. Soon he was hunted by the late Mr. Chang Chieh, the topmost kungfu movie director of that period, and became his kungfu technical director in six kungfu movies. Also, he rendered the service to make many kungfu films and TV series for other independent film production companies.

Although Professor Leung Ting's WingTsun Kungfu has been spread all over the world, he is now re-entering the TV and movie production arena for the further promotion of Chinese kungfu. Currently, he completed the self-compiled and self-directed *"It's a Mad, Mad, Mad, Mad Kungfu World"* kungfu movie. Another movie *"Behind the Personages, the Miracles and the Crooks"* is already half finished. The plan is to shoot some extended television series like *"Dr Leung Jan, the Fighting King of WingTsun"* and *"Compendium of Kungfu".*

Below: In winter 1969, Sifu Leung Ting organized the first "WingTsun Kungfu Demonstration and Chi-Sau Tournament" at the Baptist College, in which he invited many his kungfu brothers as well as great kungfu masters from various kungfu styles. This was also the first and only time that Great Grandmaster Yip Man attended such an open WingTsun demonstration organized by his followers.

From left to right: ① Sifu Wong Chu (黃柱), ② Sifu Ku Sang (古生), ③ Sifu Leung Wah (梁華) of the Hung Gar style, ④ Sifu Wong Chang (王燦) of the Mok Gar style, ⑤ Mr Tang Sang (鄧生), ⑥ Great Grandmaster Yip Man (葉問宗師), ⑦ Sifu Leung Ting (梁挺), ⑧ Mr. Lee Tat Bong (李達邦), ⑨ Sifu Yip Tin Tak (葉天德) of the Tao Style, ⑩ Sifu Bo Kin Wah (布建華), ⑪ Sifu Mak Keung (麥強). *(* Those having no special indication on their kungfu styles are Wing Tsun / Wing Chun people)*

The Background and Theory of ——

CHUM-KIU

THE NAME AND ITS CONNOTATION

*C**hum-Kiu** is the intermediate set of WingTsun kungfu, which should normally be learnt after the Siu-Nim-Tau set. As its name implies, "Chum-Kiu"*（尋橋）*means the techniques aiming at "**seeking the bridge-arms*** of the opponent".* It is however regarded by some Wing Chun people of the other branches as the *"Sinking-Bridge"*（沉橋）. This is actually a misunderstanding of its real meaning due to the two Chinese characters "尋" and "沉" in Cantonese are of the same pronunciation. In addition, the deeper meaning of Chum-Kiu says that the practitioner is to learn how to **look for a "bridge"** between him and his opponent so he can easily detect the directions of attacks from his opponent. *(* Chinese martial artists customarily call their arms as "bridges"（橋）or "bridge-arms"（橋手）; due to the reason that when two persons are fighting, their arms become the "bridge" of both.)*

Learning martial arts is to learn how to keep from being hurt by an enemy. Although a person can hurt his enemy, if he cannot prevent himself from being hurt in a fight, he would just be one of the two losers in that fight! The secret of defense relies on *"how well you can protect yourself BEFORE being attacked."* If you cannot even "find out" which part of your body will be attacked by your opponent before his punch lands on your body, it would be hard for you "not to be hit". Once a WT practitioner finds out EXACTLY the direction of the opponent's attacking movement, he can then dissolve this attacking movement much easier. *"Seeking a bridge"* therefore becomes necessary. Therefore the name *"Chum-Kiu"* bears this meaning.

The Chum-Kiu set consists mainly of defending techniques, especially *Bong-Sau* (Wing-arms); say, the *Juen-ma Bong-sau* (轉馬膀手 or Turning-stance Wing-arm), *Dap-bo Bong-sau* (踏步膀手 or Side-stepping Wing-arm) and *Dai Bong-sau* (低膀手 or Lower Wing-arm), account for almost 60% of the whole set. As for those techniques like *Chuen-Kiu* (穿橋 or "Piercing arm"), *Lan-sau* (攔手 or "Bar-arm"), *Man-sau* (問手 or "Inquisitive-arm") and *Jark-sun Gum-sau* (側身撳手 or "Sideward Pinning-hand"), occupy no more than 40% of the set. The function of most of these techniques is "to seek and to stop the bridge-arm of the opponent".

8

IMPORTANT POINTS FOR PRACTICE

When practicing Chum-Kiu, a practitioner should correctly master all the movements. A WingTsun expert should perform the Chum-Kiu set with a decorous attitude yet unadorned; when doing stepping and turning, the stance should be stable and not unwieldy; the punches and kicks should be powerful but not stiff; all the movements should be agile but precise. During pauses between techniques, the whole body should look staid yet not clumsy.

Further, a practitioner must keep both hands coordinated to defend the upper and middle part of the body. His elbows should sink down and the shoulders droop*. *(* Please refer to motto "The Sinking Elbows and Drooping Shoulders" described in the book "Siu-Nim-Tau")* Both knees should be interlocked in all circumstances so as to protect the lower body from being attacked by surprise*. *(* Please refer to "About the Essential points" in "Siu-Nim-Tau")* When turning or kicking, both the shoulders should look immovable*. *(*The kicking techniques in WingTsun are distinct from all the other martial arts. A good WingTsun practitioner is trained not to show any small dropping of any side of his shoulder when launching a kick so his opponent is never alerted to see that the WT practitioner is going to kick him.)*

THREE KICKING TECHNIQUES AND THREE PUNCHING TECHNIQUES

There are three punching techniques; say, the *Jik-sin-chung-kuen* (直線衝拳 or Frontal Thrusting-punch), the *Chau-chong-kuen* (抽撞拳 or "Lifting-punch") and the *Til-kiu-chung-kuen* (跳橋衝拳 or Jumping Thrusting-punch). The jumping thrusting-punch is derived from the Frontal Thrusting-punch and is therefore regarded as a similar technique.

There are also three kicking techniques in Chum-Kiu in the Leung Ting WingTsun™ system; the *Wang-chang-guek* (橫撐腳 or "Side Thrusting-kick"*), *Jik-chang-guek* (直撐腳 or "Frontal Thrusting-kick", alias *Ching-sun Chang-guek* 正身撐腳 or in short, 正身腳 *Ching-sun-guek*) and the *Che-chang-guek* (斜撐腳 or "Slant Thrusting-kick"). *(*For Side Thrusting-kick please refer to the following paragraphs)*

DIFFERENT FROM THE YIP MAN STYLE

The three kicking techniques passed down by the late Grandmaster Yip Man are not exactly the same. They were respectively: the <u>*Lan-sau*</u> with *Jik-chang-guek* (攔手直撐腳 or Bar-arm with Frontal Thrusting-kick); then repeat the Frontal Thrusting-kick with <u>fists placing at both sides of the chest</u>; and finally a left *Che-chang-guek* (斜撐腳 or "Slant Thrusting-kick"*) before the *Gum-sau* movements. *(*Che-chang-guek is also known as Juen-sun-chang-guek* 轉身撐腳 or "Turning Thrusting-kick"; or *Che-gwa-guek* 斜掛腳 or "Side Hanging-kick" by some Wing Chun people)*

9

DIFFERENT FROM PAST TO PRESENT?

I have no clear idea if the Chum-Kiu set learned by Great Grandmaster Yip Man in Foshan in the olden days and those he taught in Hong Kong had been modified. But, the Chum-Kiu set demonstrated by his students in Foshan (佛山 or Fatshan in Cantonese) seems not too much different from what he taught in Hong Kong.

According to my search and study on the origin of WingTsun for many years, the traditional Chum-Kiu set in Dr Leung Jan's period "probably" was not exactly the same as what we are practicing today. The ancient Chum-Kiu set, just like its original principle, should include the above "three DIFFERENT kicking techniques" as in the ancient manuscripts by some other Wing Chun people.

SIMPLICITY IN WINGTSUN SETS

The reason is very simple. First with the understanding that there are many kungfu styles claiming that they have lots of boxing sets; whereas most of the movements in their sets are actually minor modifications of a certain similar movements in different sequences and positions. Sometimes they mix up movements of different sets and add in a few new movements then give this newly formed sequence a new name so as to make it look like a new boxing set.

Since knowing the erroneous thinking of the traditional kungfu masters, our founder thought to create the Wing Tsun sets in a completely different format with a concise and logical order through simplicity to profundity rather than to create twenty or thirty sets with similar movements. In this way, many impractical and unnecessary movements were omitted in the sets. Even the most crucial techniques are repeated for one more time on either side *(e.g. the Bong-sau, turning-stances and sideling steps sequences)*.

All the sets of the Wing Tsun system were founded with this train of thought. The Frontal Thrusting-kick and Side Thrusting-kick are the most important techniques in the three basic kicking techniques of Wing Tsun. By contrast, the Slant Thrusting-kick is rarely used. According to the Wing Tsun logical thinking, why would even the Slant Thrusting-kick be put into the boxing set but not the more frequently used Side Thrusting-kick?

I suppose that it may be due to the *"Bar-arm with a Side Thrusting-kick"* movement, in which the sole of the kicking leg is just comparatively horizontal to the side, looked quite similar to the *"Bar-arm with a Frontal Thrusting-kick"*. If an instructor of a certain generation taught his student the Chum-Kiu set hastily, the student might misunderstand that they belonged to the same kicking format.

INFORMATION COLLECTION FOR VERIFICATION

Some years ago, I coincidentally obtained some materials to verify that there were only three basic kicking movements passed on in most Wing Chun branches.

Besides, there are also *said to be:* Saam-Sau (三手 or "Three Hand Techniques"), *Saam-Kuen* (三拳 or "Three Punching Techniques"), *Saam-Chang* (三掌 or "Three Palm-strike Techniques"), *Saam-Jarn* (三睜 or "Three Elbow-strike Techniques") and *Saam-Guek* (三腳 or "Three Kicking Techniques") in the traditional Wing Tsun (Wing Chun) system. All of them are fundamental techniques from which all the fighting techniques are transmuted. *(*For the detailed explanation of the above terms, please refer to my new book "The last page of WingTsun — Mottoes & Concepts".)*

Through the analysis on the *Muk-Yan-Chong-Fat* (木人樁法 or "Wooden Dummy Techniques") taught by the late Great Grandmaster Yip Man in Foshan , we can conclude that there were only three kicking movements in WingTsun at that time *(assuming his Foshan students had not modified their movements).*

INSPIRATION BY DIFFERENT STYLES WITH THE SAME SOURCE

When I was in West Berlin in 1977, I eye-witnessed a private demonstration of the Ling Lom (Flying Monkey) style martial arts by Mr Sunthus Suspasturpong, a Thai Boxing Champion as well as the headman of European Thai Boxing headquarters at that period. He said that the Flying Monkey style was a kind of mysterious kungfu derived from provinces of Szechwan and Yunnan. In a manuscript *"The Origin of WingTsun"* written by the late Grandmaster Yip Man*, it is mentioned that the Buddhist Mistress Ng Mui created a new fighting system on the border between the provinces of Szechwan and Yunnan and later passed it to Yim Wing Tsun *(some spell her name as "Yim Wing Chun").* I was suddenly enlightened after this kungfu communication in Berlin. The clue about the story was verified by then. *(* Please refer to the book "Roots of Wing Tsun" or "Wing Tsun Kuen" for details)*

Meanwhile, I also learned that the basic techniques of the Flying Monkey style consisted of *"Three Punching Techniques", "Three Palm-strike Techniques"* and *"Three Kicking Techniques".* I had even made fun with Mr Suspasturpong by telling him that: *"Fortunately we have eight kicking techniques! Ha, ha…"*

In fact, at that time I was ignorant of the fact that the traditional Wing Tsun kungfu system actually consisted of only three kicks.

11

Upper: Sunthus demonstrating movements of the Flying Monkey style, in which many techniques are similar to those of Wing Tsun.

Lower: The techniques demonstrated above are similar to the *"Crossed Gaun-sau"* in the beginning of all the sets of WingTsun and the *"Long-bridge Pinning-hands"* of the Siu Nim Tau set.

MORE DISCOVERIES BY TRACING THE ROOTS

At the time I learned advanced techniques from Great Grandmaster Yip Man, I was told about the terms such as *"Saam-Chang"* and *"Saam-Kuen"*. Once he even explained and demonstrated to me the *"Saam-Fan-Chang"* (三瓣掌 or "Three leafs of Palms"*) and *"Sep-Gee-Chang* (十字掌 or "Crossed Palms"). What a pity at that time I was just too cursory on what he said and did not keep asking him more about the traditional aspects.

In the early 80's, I obtained a manuscript on the detailed descriptions about Wing Chun kungfu of the past. I also met some old people of other Wing Chun branches. The roots and development of Wing Tsun soon draw my attention. After many more years, I obtained more and more Wing Chun manuscripts, handwriting paper or notes from different people of other Wing Chun schools. With continuous research, I was told a lot of unknown stories, unusual pieces of information and collected the similarities and differences of techniques and thinking between different Wing Chun branches. Some are authentic, some fabricated, some are totally illogical and yet some are half-true and half-false. No matter how, I am glad to have collected numerous materials and information from those people that really enriches my own WingTsun accomplishments. The "Side Thrusting-kick" is among the findings.

ALTERATION OF KICKING MOVEMENTS

After a two-year study, discussions and experiments on new and old kicking movements, I finally decided to change the first sequence of kicking movements in Chum-Kiu back into Side Thrusting-Kick. My reasons are as follows:

1   All three of the basic kicking techniques would be included in the Chum-Kiu set;

2   To save more time —— It takes three movements from Bar-arm, turning-stance and then a frontal thrusting-kick. If I apply a Bar-arm with a side thrusting-kick, I only need two movements. After kicking, as my body is still facing frontally, I need not to turn back to the front side for dealing with another enemy at the front. For this reason, I actually save two movements if I apply a side thrusting-kick instead.

WHO CARES ABOUT "TRADITION"?

Putting the Side Thrusting-kicks into the Chum-Kiu set doesn't mean that I have attempted to restore the so-called "tradition" or "observe the authenticity". I don't care whether the Side Thrusting-kick was really included in traditional Chum-Kiu set or not. **The most important thing is that if you are knocked out in a fight, who cares how traditional you are?**

A — F: THE LATE GREAT GRANDMASTER YIP MAN DEMONSTRATING THE MIDDLE SECTION OF THE CHUM-KIU SET:
Sequence started from Bar-arm (A), Frontal Thrusting-kick (B), Stepping Sideling Bong-sau (C — D), Crossed Tan-sau (E) to Lifting-punch (F). *(Note: Repeated movements are omitted in this series.)*

Please pay attention that unlike the most common mistakes many of his students make, Grandmaster Yip Man did not withdraw his foot after kicking but stepped down on the same place (B — C). When applying the Sideling Bong-sau, his Wu-sau was placed at the center of the chest (D). When applying the Crossed Tan-sau, both of his forearms did not drop down to the waist's level but were in front of his chest (E).

OTHER CHANGES

Moreover, I have added two more Jumping-punches after the Sideling Gum-sau. *(There was only one Jumping punch in Chum-Kiu set passed down by Grandmaster Yip Man.)*

In the past, WingTsun kungfu was mostly used to deal with martial artists practicing Southern Shaolin (南少林 or *"Nam Siu Lam"* in Cantonese), who usually applied groin-kicks to attack the groins of their opponents. If someone is good at protecting the lower level of the body and good at applying the "Close-Rang Pursuing-Attack" (迫步貼打 or *"Bik-Bo-Tip-Da"* in Cantonese) fighting tactic, he doesn't actually need to use the Sideling Gum-Sau for blocking. However, we are now often facing the opponents from karate, taekwondo, kickboxing, Thai boxing or something else. They are skillful at kicking to the high and low levels with roundhouse kicks and snap-kicks. Sideling Gum-sau and Jumping Punches thus become the best combination to deal with these opponents.

Thousands of followers converted from other martial arts to WingTsun. Many of them are experts in kicking. As in this photo, the chief combat training officer of SEK Special police of Germany (left), before learning WingTsun, was a three-time European karate champion and now a 4th Level WingTsun instructor. The one at the left side of Prof Leung is also a WingTsun combat instructor of special police.

Below: Photo taken in 2002 when Prof Leung teaching the Hungarian soldiers to pound their enemies in a split second with lethal techniques. The one doing demonstration is Master Széll Gábor, a grand-student of Leung and the bare-handed combat instructor of the Special Corps in the Hungarian military.

尋 橋 拳 譜

CHUM-KIU — The Arm-Seeking Set

Demonstrated by
Great Master Cheng Chuen Fun
(9th Level MOA)

Setting Up the *Yee-Gee-Kim-Yeung-Ma* (1 — 4)

Relax. Stand straight, feet together, arms by your sides. Pull the fists to your armpit, parallel to nipple line. Bend your knees allowing your upper body to sink vertically downward. Using the heels as pivots, turn your feet outward as far as possible. Then using the tiptoes of your feet as pivots, turn your heels outward until both feet form an equilateral angle *(60° to each other)* on the ground. This is the *Yee-Gee-Kim-Yeung-Ma* (Character 'Two' Adduction Stance).

Gow-cha Gaun-sau — Kwun-sau — Gow-cha Tan-sau (5 — 8) Place the left hand on the right hand and cut down quickly to form the *Gow-cha Gaun-sau* (Crossed Splitting-arms). Roll both hands up along the body with the *Kwun-sau* (Rotating-arms) movement and finally form the *Gow-cha Tan-sau* (Crossed Palm-up arm) pose .

18

Sau-kuen **(Withdrawal of Fists) (5 — 9)** After the Crossed *Tan-sau* movement, withdraw the fists to the armpits.

Left *Yat-gee-chung-kuen – Huen-sau — Sau-kuen* (10—16)

Launch a left *Yat-gee-chung-kuen* (Character 'Sun' Thrusting-punch or "Thrusting-punch" for short). When the arm is fully extended, open the palm upward and circle it inwards. This is the *Huen-sau* (Circling-hand) movement. Withdraw the fist.

Right Character 'Sun' Thrusting-punch — Circling-hand — Withdrawal of the fist (17 — 23)

Chuen-Kiu (Piercing-arms) (24 — 26)

First place both hands in front of the chest at about one-fist distance. Stop for a second, then suddenly, thrust both arms out up to the upper level with full strength like an explosion.

Three-time *Pie-jam* (Elbow-hacking) Movements to both sides (27 — 29)
Turn to the left side and, simultaneously, bend both arms with the left arm over the right. Then turn to the right side, and finally turn back to the left side again.

Shang Fook-sau & Three-time Left & Right Pak-sau (30 — 33)

Stretch out both arms with palms facing the ground. Slap the right palm at the bend of the left arm when it turns to a *Tan-sau*. Perform this movement three times.

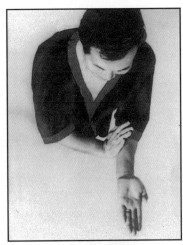

Left: Top shot of *Shang Fook-sau*
(雙伏手 or Double Bridge-on arms)

Right: Top shot of *Pak-sau*
(拍手 or Slapping-hand)

Ching-cheung (Erect Palm) & *Wu-sau* (Protective-arm) (34 — 36)

Thrust the right palm forward and place the left palm in front of the chest to form a *Wu-sau*. Then make a left palm-strike and place the right palm in front of the chest. Finally, make a right palm-strike once more and draw the left fist back to the armpit.

Juen-ma Lan-Sau — Gow-cha Tan-Sau & Juen-ma Bong-sau for 3 times (37 — 43) Turn to the right and bend the right arm to form a *Lan-sau* (Bar-arm) at the same time. Place both hands in front of the chest to form *Gow-cha Tan-sau* (Crossed Tan-sau). Turn to the front to make a Sideling *Bong-sau*. Repeat the above sequence for a total of three times. *(*"Juen-ma" 轉馬 in Chinese means "Turning-stance")*

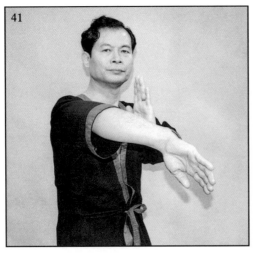

Photo: Medium Shot of the Right Jark-sun Bong-Sau

Please note that when applying the right *Jark-sun* Bong-sau (側身膀手 or "Sideling Wing-arm"), the left arm should make a *Wu-sau* (護手 or "Protective-arm") posing at the center of the chest at a distance facing the elbow-joint of the Bong-sau.

***Lan-Sau* (Bar-arm) & *Til-kiu Chung-kuen* (Jumping Thrusting Punch) (44 — 46)** After the last Lan-sau movement, place the left fist in front of the chest at a palm's distance. Punch it over the right forearm heading to the face of an imaginary opponent; at the same time withdraw the right fist to the armpit.

28

Fat-Sau **(Whisking-arm) (47)**

After the left arm is totally straightened, stop for a second, then suddenly whisk the left arm to the right (as shown) like a whip. Simultaneously, turn the whole body back to the frontal side again with this *Fat-sau* (Whisking-arm) movement.

Fook-sau — Jut-sau — Tut-sau (48 — 50)

Withdraw the left hand from the left side and pose a *Fook-sau* in front of the chest. Put the right hand on the bend of the left arm. Now slip it out over the left arm to make a *Da-ngan-sau* (Eye-thrusting) movement. Make a *Jut-sau* action and draw back the left arm simultaneously when the right arm is thrusting outward.

30

Huen-sau & _Sau-kuen_ (51 — 54) When the right arm is totally extended, execute a circling movement _(Huen-sau)_. Then draw the fist back to the armpit position _(Sau-kuen)_.

Three-time *Pie-jarn* (Elbow-hacking) movements of the opposite sides (55 — 59) Repeat the previous movements but on the opposite sides.

32

Shang Fook-sau **(Bridge-on arm) &** ***Pak-Sau*** **(Slapping-hand) of the opposite sides (60 — 63)** Repeat the previous movements but on the opposite sides.

Three-time *Ching-cheung* **(Erect-palm) &** *Wu-sau* **(Protective-arm) of the opposite sides (64 — 66)** Repeat the previous sequences on the opposite sides.

Three-time *Lan-sau* (Bar-arm), *Gow-cha Tan-sau* (Crossed Palm-up arm) and *Juen-ma Bong-sau* (Turning-stance Wing-arm) of the opposite sides (67 — 73) Repeat the previous movements on the opposite sides.

Lan-Sau (Bar-arm) & _Til-kiu Chung-kuen_ (Jumping Thrusting-punch) — _Fat-sau_ (Whisking-arm) of the opposite sides (74 — 76)
Repeat the previous movements on the opposite sides.

Fook-sau (Bridge-on arm) — _Tut-sau_ (Freeing-arm) — _Huen-sau_ (Circling-hand) & _Sau-kuen_ (Withdrawal of the fist) (77 — 84) Repeat the previous movements on the opposite side.

***Jor Com-lan* (Left Grappling and Barricading-arm) (85 — 86)** Open the left hand wide with four fingers opposite to the thumb like a crescent moon. Push the left hand to the right and, at the same time and make a grasping action (as shown). Finally the hand is at a palm's distance in front of the right shoulder.

Jor Com-lan (Continued) (87)

Draw the left arm to the left side and shift the weight of the upper body onto the right leg simultaneously. The left arm is then posed as a *Lan-sau* horizontally lying at the left-hand side at the shoulder height.

Wang Chang-guek **(Side Thrusting-Kick) (88 — 89)** Thrust the left leg horizontally to the left with full strength. The upper body should not move even slightly while kicking. When the leg is fully extended, step down, placing the foot where it reaches. Right after the foot has touched the floor, immediately make a step by dragging the whole body to the left side with the knee-force of the left leg.

Wang-dap-bo Bong-sau **(Side-stepping Wing-sau) &** ***Gow-cha Tan-sau***
(Crossed Palm-up arm) (90 — 4) Make a Sideling *Bong-sau* when stepping to
the left side; place the right *Wu-sau* in front of the chest. Stop for a second; then
change both arms to *Gow-cha Tan-sau*. Perform this sequence a total of three times.

Chau-chong-kuen **(Lifting-punch) (95)** After the third *Dap-bo Bong-sau* (Stepping Wing-arm), turning to the left and launch a lifting-punch at the same time.

Fook-sau – Tut-sau – Huen-sau & Sau-kuen (96 — 102) Turn the body to the front again. Pose the right arm as a *Fook-sau* (Bridge-on arm) and thrust the left-hand out over the joint of the right arm. This is the *Da-ngan-sau* (Eye-thrusting hand) movement. Execute a Circling-hand before withdrawal of the fist *(Sau-kuen)*.

Side Thrusting-kick to the Right (103 — 105)
Launch the *Wang-chang-guek* (Side Thrusting-kick) with the right leg.

Dap-bo Bong-sau (Stepping Wing-arm) & Lifting Punch to the Right (106 — 112) Repeat the above sequence on the right side.

Fook-sau **(Bridge-on arm)** — ***Tut-sau*** **(Freeing-arm)** — ***Huen-sau*** **(Circling-hand)** **&** ***Sau-kuen*** **(Withdrawal of the fist)** **(112 — 119)**
Repeat the above sequence but on the opposite side.

Juen-ma **(Turning-stance)** — ***Ching-sun-guek*** **(Frontal Thrusting-kick) (120 — 122)** Turn to the left. Launch a Frontal Thrusting-kick horizontally to the left side with the foot straight up. The shoulders should not move slightly when kicking.

3-time *Dap-bo Dai-bong-sau* and *Shang Tan-sau* (122 — 127) Step down the left foot to where it reaches. Make a step to the left side by dragging the whole body forwards. Turn both arms into Lower *Bong-sau* while stepping. Turn to Double *Tan-sau* after the step. Repeat the Bong and Tan sequence for a total of three times.

Man-sau (128 — 129) Step the left foot forwards after the third _Dai-Bong-sau_ movement. Then step the right foot forwards and lift up both arms to form the _Man-sau_ (Inquisitive-arms) movement, with the back of both hands pressing close together and fingers facing upward and, at the same time closing up both feet.

Shang Jut-sau — Shang Tui-cheung (130 — 132) Lower the arms and form the Shang Jut-sau (Double Jerk-hands) movement by the power exerted from the elbows. Thrust both palms forwards. This is the Shang Tui-cheung (Double Erect-palm strike) movement.

51

Oi-huen-sau (External Circling-hands) — ***Sau-kuen*** — ***Dao-dap-bo***
(Withdrawal step) (133 — 137) After fully extending both arms, droop the hands
down and circle both hands upward from inside to outside. Withdraw the fists.
Then step backwards with the right foot. Turn 180° from the left to the right side.

***Juen-ma* (Turning-stance) to the right — *Ching-sun-guek* (Frontal Thrusting-kick) *Dap-bo Dai-bong-sau* (137 — 141)** Repeat the sequence as in pictures #120 to 123 but on the opposite side.

The second & third time of *Dap-bo Dai-bong-sau* and *Shang Tan-sau* movements — *Man-sau* (Inquisitive arms) (143 — 147)
Repeat the above sequence but on the opposite side.

Double Jerking-hands — Double Thrusting-palms — External Circling-hands — Withdrawal of fists (144 — 155) Repeat the sequence as in pictures #130 to 136 but on the opposite side. Pay attention to the close-ups of the External Circling-hands *(Oi-huen-sau)* movements from #151 to 153.

Juen-ma (Stance-turning) — ***Che-chang-guek*** (Slant Thrusting-kick)
(156 — 157) Keep both fists beneath the armpits. Turn both soles at the original place until the upper body is facing the front. Raise the left leg and make a slant thrusting-kick to the left side at full stretch.

Jark-sau Gum-sau **(Sideling Pinning-hand) (158 — 160)** When the left foot steps on the ground, the right foot is brought close to form a Sideling stance *(Jark-sun-ma)*. Make a downward pinning-hand with the left palm, followed by that of the right palm. Then a third time for the left hand.

***Jark-sun Gum-sau* followed by *Til-kiu Chung-kuen* (161 — 165)** At the
end of the third Pinning-hand movement, change the left palm to a fist and launch
an upward-forward thrusting punch aiming to the "face" level to make a *"Til-kiu
chung-kuen"* or "Jumping Thrusting-punch", an instantaneous counterattack
without changing a hand. Perform this movement for a total of three times.

Kiu-Dai Chung-kuen **(Thrusting-punch from Underneath) (166 —
167)** After the left arm is fully extended, thrust the right punch forward beneath the
left arm. This is the so-called *"Kiu-Dai Chung-kuen"* or, more correctly translated
as, "the Thrusting-punch from the bottom of the bridge-arm".

Lin-wan Chung-kuen **(Chain-punches) (168 — 171)** At the full stretch of
the right punch, launch a left thrusting-punch out over the right arm. Meanwhile,
withdraw the elbow of the right arm to the chest. Do these continuous punching
movements as swiftly as possible.

Huen-sau (Circling-hand) — ***Su-kuen*** (Withdrawal of the fist) (172 — 177) After several punches, finish up the chain-punches with the left arm. Make a circling-hand movement and then withdraw the fist.

Sau-sik (Closing the set) (178)

Stand up. Move the left leg to the right leg and close them together. The whole bare-hand set is now completed.

END

APPLICATION & ANALYSIS OF THE MOVEMENTS

CHUEN-KIU (穿橋 or **Piercing-arms**)

"Chuen-kiu" or "Piercing-arms" is the first movement after the *Gow-cha Gaun-sau** (Crossed Splitting arm) and the left and right Thrusting punches* in the Chum-Kiu set. *(* Please refer to the book "Siu-Nim-Tau" for details.)*

"Chuen-kiu" is used to make both arms pierce through the arms of the opponent. It is not only applied for dealing with those attacking movements such as double-hooked punches (alias "horn-punches") but pre-fighting postures with two forearms posing vertically adjacent to either side of the head as done by the full-contact and Thai boxing fighters.

As this movement normally goes with the Eye-thrusting attack, it is sometimes called "Double Eye-thrusting hands" or *"Shang Da-ngan-sau* (雙打眼手). The Eye-thrusting hand in WingTsun is different from the eye-jabbing techniques of other martial-art styles. Instead of using the fingers to jab the eyes of our opponent, we thrust the eyes with our thumbs. The thumb is short but much stronger than the four other fingers added together. Sometimes, we may use the four fingers to clinch the cheek of the opponent in order to keep him from moving back.

Traditionally, our masters of higher generations did not want to teach this technique to their ordinary students due to its venomous purpose. This is the reason there are not too many people who really know the application of this technique. The purpose of publishing the eye-thrusting hand here is to show the completeness of the Chum-Kiu set. I hereby, would like to emphatically warn practitioners to refrain from applying this dangerous movement in fighting.

Demonstrators:
Sifu Carson Lau (Left)

Assistant Instructor
Bjorn Sandelin (Right)

Diagram A — C:

A (left) is confronting **B** face to face. When **B** launches a double hook-punch to attack **A** on the temples, **A** immediately applies a *Chuen-Kiu* movement by thrusting both arms upwards. In the mean time, **A** applies the Eye-thrusting hands to jab both thumbs into the eyes of **B**. By doing this, **B**'s attack is also dissolved. This is the so-called "To counter an attack by an attack" （以打為消）fighting tactic of WingTsun.

BELOW:
A close-up shot showing the angles between the WingTsun practitioner and his opponent when the former counters with an Eye-thrusting Technique

JOR - YAU LAN-SAU (左右攔手 or **Left & Right Bar-arms**)
Alias "CHIN HAU PIE-JAAN" (前後批睜 or **Forward & Backward Horizontal Elbow-hacking**)

Most of the karate, taekwondo or kungfu fighters find it very difficult get rid of their opponent when being powerfully clinched. A WingTsun expert, however, can easily dissolve this problem. *Lan-sau* (攔手 or "Bar-arm") in Chum-Kiu is one of the "double-movements"*. They can be subdivided into the *"Chin-Pie-Jarn"* (Forward horizontal elbow-hacking) and the *"Hau-Pie-Jarn"* (Backward horizontal elbow hacking) to deal with powerful clinches under different situations.

Chin-Pie-Jarn (前批睜) is also called *"Shun-Pie-Jarn"* (順批睜 or "Onward elbow-hacking"). For example, when posing a right bar-arm in front of the chest and the body is turning from right to left, the ulna (the outer bone of forearm) is hacking to the left with a turning movement. The ulna is quite flat and hard, which can hurt the opponent as if using the blade of a knife to cut an object.

The *Hau-Pie-Jarn* (後批睜), alias the *"Yik-pie-jarn"* (逆批睜 or "Reverse elbow-hacking") movement, is performed by turning to the opposite side with a right bar-arm.

Shun-Pie-Jarn can be applied to "crosscut" the neck, the throat, the head, the eye and even the breastbone of the opponent.

Yik-Pie-Jarn, instead of "cutting", is mostly applied as a way of "crashing" on the side or the back of the neck.

(* Please refers to "Double-movements" of the book "WingTsun Kuen" for details)

65

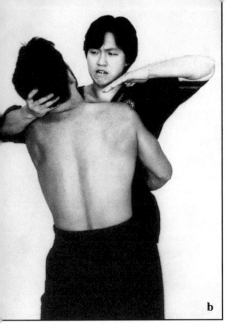

Diagram a — d:

A is clinched by **B** at the waist and is lifted above the ground.

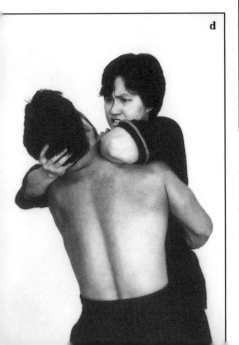

A immediately applies a *Shun-Pie-Jarn* by bending his left forearm to horizontally hack **B**'s neck with a twisting movement of the upper body. Being attacked, **B** has no choice but to give up the powerful clinch.

Application of the
Yik-Pie-Jarn:

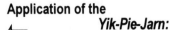

B, with his head leaning tightly against the right armpit of **A**, strongly clinches his opponent at the chest.

Under such a circumstance, **A** is not able to apply punches or even an Onward Elbow-hacking technique to counter **B**.

Hence **A** applies a *Yik-pie-jarn* or "Reverse Elbow-hacking" movement to strike **B** on the back of the neck with his elbow as his upper body turns.

Demonstrators:

Assistant Instructor
Lam Lap Chung (A)

Sifu Christopher Collins (B)

PAK-SAU (拍手 or **Slapping-hand**)

Most of the Wing Chun people misunderstand the real function of the *Pak-sau* movement in Chum-Kiu. They believe that they can break their opponent's arm with the following technique: *"while an opponent is attacking a WC practitioner with a straight punch, traps the opponent's arm by laying it on his forearm and slaps it upwards with the lifting palm from underneath, spontaneously, applying another palm to slap on the wrist of the opponent so as to break it."* **Unfortunately this is not practical at all!** The reasons are explained in the following points:

1: No one is that stupid to stretch out his arm entirely and let his opponent break it in a fight. *(Unless he is your student and it is you who asked for it!)*

2: Even if the opponent has really stretched out one arm, he still can launch another punch to attack you. It would be bad luck that you would, in fact, not have a "third" arm to deal with his coming punch because both your arms have been occupied to trap his single, outstretched arm.

3: In fact, it is not easy to break somebody's arm by using the "slapping-hand" movement, even if he gives you the chance to do it.

In the past 30 years, I have invited volunteers hundred times to try to break my arm in open kungfu shows and seminars all over the world. It proves that slapping hand or any kind of the so-called "arm-breaking" techniques cannot break my arm even though I totally straightened my arm and did nothing. *(*I confess that I was applying the WingTsun "unloading force" techniques in the show yet it looks like I did nothing.)*

Lower: In 1999, Grandmaster Leung Ting invited one of the local policemen, who was also a black-belt karateka, to try to break his arm in an open seminar when Leung was teaching the special force in India.

Before I became a close-door student of the late Grandmaster Yip Man, I had learned the "arm-breaking" technique from my first instructor in the above method. After practicing this movement with great effort for several months, I finally gave up the idea due to its entirely impractical usage. Then I looked for a better method for years. It was not until the early 80s, in an old manuscript recorded by a Wing Chun

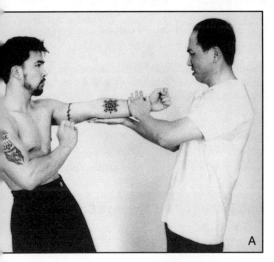

master during Dr Leung Jan's period, that I found out the most reasonable explanation on the application of this technique. It soon reminded me of a similar movement shown by the late Grandmaster Yip Man while doing *Chi-Sau* with me during a lesson. With the "half-twisting-half-slapping" movement, it should be possible to dislocate the joint of the opponent's arm.

WRONG TECHNIQUE:

Please pay attention to the fact that the so-called "Slapping-hand" technique shown here is actually a very bad technique. The attempt to break the arm of the opponent as done by most of the Wing Chun practitioners on the right side, regardless of its ineffectiveness, turns out to be a big opportunity for the opponent to counter with another hand.

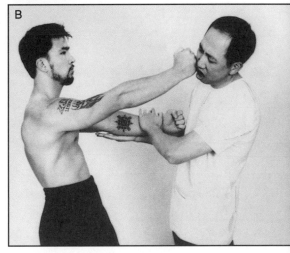

69

Two Practical Ways of Slapping-Hands

There are two different applications for the Slapping-hands. The method illustrated below is the most common way of Slapping-hand technique applied in *Chi-sau* drills. *(Diagram A — E)*

The second method — the *Pak-jarn-sau* — technique can be found on *page 75.*

INDOOR-AREA SLAPPING-HAND IN CHI-SAU

Diagram A — E:

A (right) and **B** are working on *Poon-Sau* (Rolling-arms) movements in the Double-arm *Chi-Sau* (Double arm clinging) drill. *(Diagram A)* While **A** changes his right *Bong-sau* (Wing-arm) into a *Tan-sau* (Palm-up arm) posture, he immediately changes his left *Fook-sau* (Bridge-on arm) into a *Pak-sau* (Slapping-hand) movement slapping to the bend of **B**'s left arm. *(Diagram B — C)* This is the *"Yat-Fook-Yee"* (一伏二) or *"Trapping two-arms by one-arm"* fighting tactic in WingTsun. *(Diagram D)* When **A** is pressing down **B**'s both arms, his right hand has changed into a Thrusting-punch landing on **B**'s chest. *(Diagram E)*

Demonstrators:

Grandmaster Leung Ting (right) **Sifu Wong Nga Chung** (left)

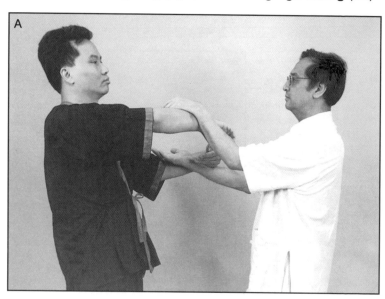

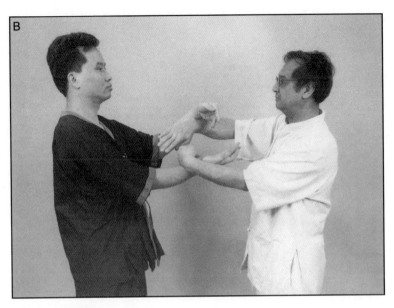

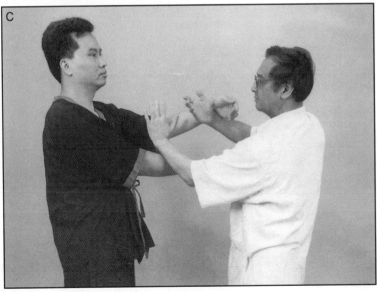

71

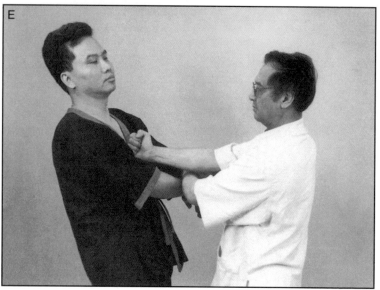

NOI-MOON PAK-SAU & CHUNG-KUEN IN REAL COMBAT (or *"Noi-Moon Pak-Da"* 內門拍打 in short)

The *Pak-sau* (Slapping-hand) and Thrusting-punch practiced in Double-arm *Chi-Sau* can be applied in real combat:

Diagram 1 — 4:
A (left) confronts **B**. **A** starts the attack by charging forward and slapping down **B**'s left wrist with the left Slapping-hand. At the same time, **A** executes a right Thrusting-punch onto **B**'s chest.

(Note: Please pay attention that when **A** is attacking **B** with a Thrusting-punch, **A**'s left forearm is pressing both arms of **B**'s strongly against his own body. Meanwhile, the wrist of **A**'s right punch-arm is also depressing **B**'s right *Wu-sau* (Protective-arm) tightly so as not to offer **B** any chance of escape or execute any dissolving movements.

Please also refer to *pg. 122* about the topic: *"Beware when applying an Indoor-area Slapping-hand Movement"* in *"About the Essential Points"*, for details)

Demonstrators:

Sifu Wong Nga Chung (left)

Sifu Yan Yiu Wing (right)

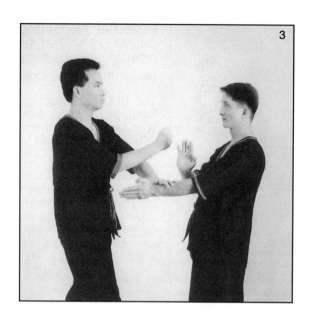

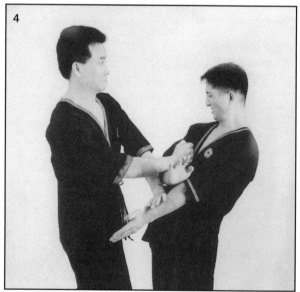

To "Break the Arm" with a *"Pak-jarn-sau"*

It was mentioned in the previous text that to slap and break the arm of the opponent with a *Pak-jarn-sau* (拍睜手 or "Elbow-slapping hand") technique according to the method stated on *Page 69* is actually impossible. However, if we can apply the technique illustrated below, it would be possible for us to execute a temporary arm-lock or, with correctly applied pressure, to even dislocate the joint of the opponent's arm, in either the Double-arm *Chi-Sau* drill or in real combat.

I have been teaching this technique in the special training programs for Special Forces, police departments and prison guards for years. It has proven to be quite practical to apply this movement in controlling law-breakers or criminals in violent situations.

THE ELBOW-SLAPPING HAND IN CHI-SAU DRILL

Diagram 1 — 3:
A (right) and **B** are exercising *Poon-Sau* (Rolling-Arms) movements in the Double-arm *Chi-Sau* (Double-arm Clinging) drill. Suddenly **B** uses his left *Fook-sau* (Bridge-on arm) to slap the left arm of **A**, and, at the same time launches a right Thrusting-punch to attack **A** on the chest; **A** wastes no time to roll up his right arm to form a *Wu-Sau* (Protective-arm) to contact **B**'s coming punch mid-way between him and his opponent.

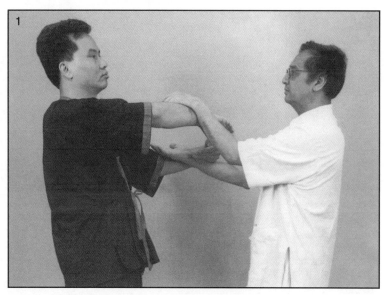

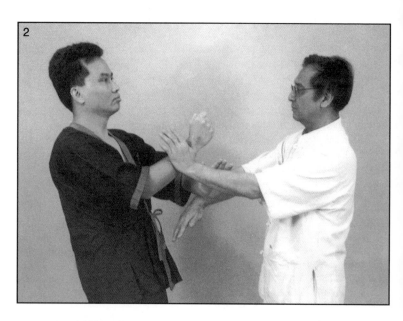

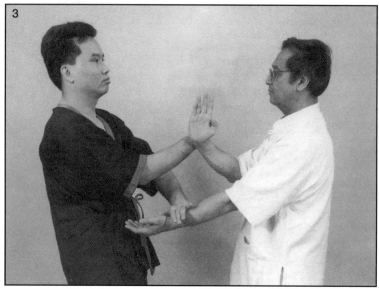

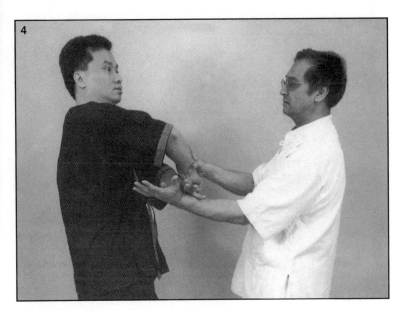

Diagram 4 — 6:
Without delay, **A** changes his *Wu-Sau* into a *Jut-Sau* (Jerk-hand) to grapple and press down **B**'s right wrist with a jerk. Simultaneously, **A** grasps **B**'s right wrist and turns the elbow over with the cooperation of his left Slapping-hand. This circling-smack-upturning power would be extremely painful to **B**.

THE THREE CHAIN PALM-STRIKING MOVEMENTS IN CHUM-KIU

The *Lin-wan Saam-cheung* (連環三掌 or "Three Chain Palm-striking" movements) in Chum-Kiu is not applied to attack the face of the opponent in combat.

When a WingTsun fighter is facing one side of his opponent in a "T-shape" position in a confrontation, it would be a good time for the WingTsun fighter to execute a Palm-strike straight to the ear of his opponent.

The principal is the same in the so-called *"Breaking a bottle with the Slapping palm"* *Chi-kung* shows. If the performer slaps the neck of the half-water-loaded glass-bottle at high speed, the sudden pressure squeezed inside will break the bottle into pieces with an explosion-like force. In the same way, a heavy palm-strike to the ear can make the opponent fall into a coma immediately. What is more, **the heavy striking can easily break the eardrum,** while a fist-strike can only hurt the outside of the ear severely. It is therefore an extremely lethal palm-striking technique. I hereby warn my readers to consider carefully before using this technique against an attacker.

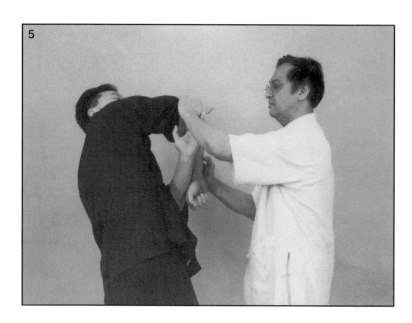

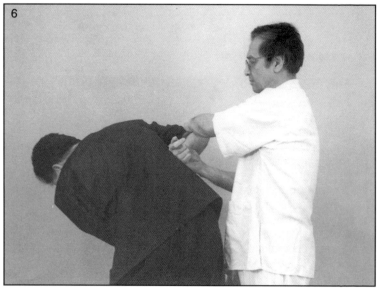

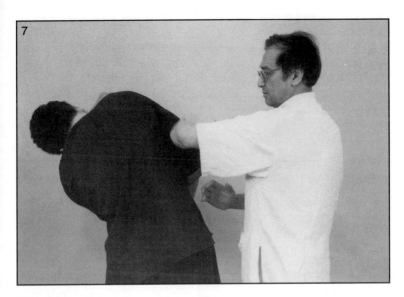

Diagram 7 — 8:
While controlling **B**'s right arm, **A** attacks **B** with a right Elect-palm strike on the ear.

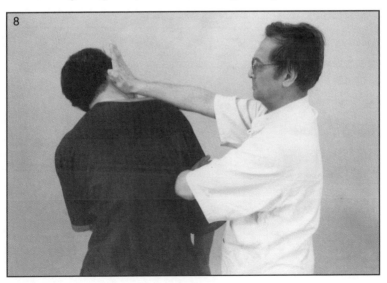

79

Elbow-slapping hand in Combat

The Elbow-slapping hand technique practiced in the Double arm *Chi-Sau* drills can be applied as a countering or even attacking movement in real combat. It can be also modified to become an effective restraining technique for law enforcement or prison officers to deal with criminals or terrorists. *(Please refer to Page 85 for details)*

Diagram 1 — 2:
A (right) is confronting **B**. While stepping forward, **B** attacks **A** with a left slapping hand on the forearm of **A** and attacks him by executing a right punch to **A**'s chest.

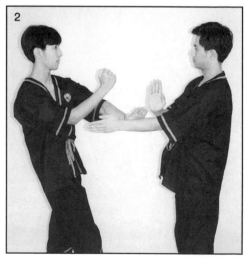

Demonstrators:

Sifu Ngai Sing Sing
(Right)

Assistant Instructor
Wong Wai Kin (Left)

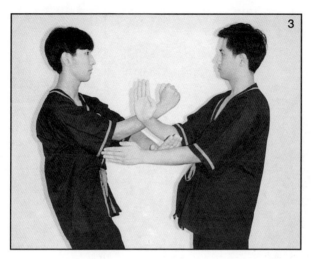

Diagram 3 — 4:
A wastes no time in turning up the right *Wu-Sau* to block **B**'s right punch. Immediately, **A** changes it into a Jerk-hand movement to jerk down **B**'s right wrist. At the same time, **A**'s left palm has already slapped the elbow of **B**'s right arm.

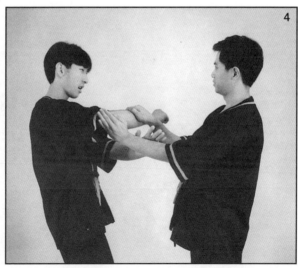

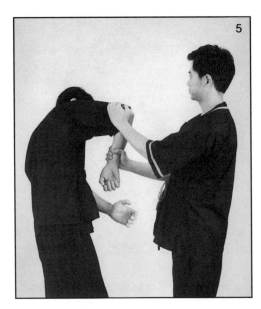

Diagram 5 — 6:

A soon grasps **B**'s right arm and overturns his elbow with assistance of the left hand twisting **B**'s arm in a clockwise direction. The violent twisting action causes **B** great pain so he is now totally under control.

TUT-SAU (脫手 or **Freeing-arm**) &
DA-NGAN-SAU (打眼手 or **Eye-thrusting hand**) SEQUENCE

Tut-sau is done before the fist-withdrawal movements in most of the individual sequences of the Chum-Kiu set. *Tut-sau* is actually a very powerful technique for counterattack. In actual application, after a WingTsun fighter applies a *Fook-sau* (Bridge-on arm) to contact the attacking arm of his opponent, he should thrust out the other hand to make a *Da-ngan-sau* over the *Fook-sau* (which is now forming a jerk-force to jerk down the opponent's arm) to attack the eye of the opponent.

In the Chum-Kiu set, the attacking-arm arm is always in an "Eye-thrusting hand" (*Da-ngan-sau*) format in the *Tut-sau* sequence. However, since the principle of WingTsun kungfu is flexible, it is not a "must" for us to always use the techniques combining *Jut-Sau* (Jerk-hand) with Eye-thrusting hand immutably in combat. Instead, we can combine a *Jut-sau* with a Thrusting-punch that is still very practical technique yet not as permanently injurious as the Eye-thrusting hand.

Please note that the *Fook-sau*, while the Thrusting-punch is traveling outward, should be turned into a *Jut-sau* so the jerk force can make the opponent lose his balance and fall forward. As a result, the forward force of the opponent would collide with the punching force of the defender so as to increase the striking power to the enemy.

This is the motto: ***"To attack the opponent by making use of his own Force"*** (借力打力) in WT fighting tactics.

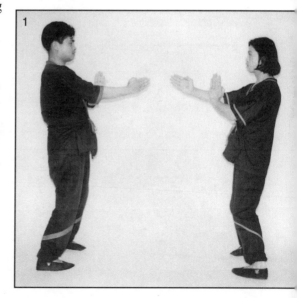

Diagram 1 — 3:
A (left) is confronting **B** with his right arm in front as a *Man-sau* (問手 or "Inquisitive-arm") and his left guarding to the rear as a *Wu-sau*. When **B** executes a right Thrusting-punch to attack **A**, **A** extends out the right *Fook-sau* to meet with **B**'s oncoming punch.

Demonstrators:
Sifu Carson Lau
(Left)

Sifu Ngan Tak Yee
(Right)

At the same time **A** is changing his right hand into a Jerk-hand movement to press down **B**'s right wrist suddenly, he attacks **B** with a left punch shooting straight over his own Jerk-hand into **B**'s chest. As **B** is losing his balance and falling forward due to the powerful jerking force exerted by **A**, he is hurt badly when the two forces *(the force of falling forward and the force of the punch)* combine to increase the impact.

A Modified Technique for Special Police to Capture a Criminal

A slight modification of the *Pak-jarn-sau* and *Fook-sau* combined together with the *Com-na-sau* (擒拿手 or "Grappling-hand") movement can form a very practical technique for swiftly capturing a dangerous criminal, barehanded. The following group of movements is listed in the "Arresting Techniques" programs for Special Forces, prison guards, police and law enforcement officials.

Demonstrators:

Sifu Ma How Nam (A)

Sifu Christopher Collins (B)

Diagram A — C:

For certain reasons Policeman **A** (right) cannot arrest **B** by drawing out his gun and pointing it towards him. He therefore pretends to be a pedestrian, lost in his own thoughts and walking close to **B** (just like a somebody not paying attention to where he is going) in the street. All of a sudden, **A** grabs **B**'s arm and uses the right wrist-bone to cut into the joint of **B**'s arm. As the joint is a very weak point, the movement hurts **B**'s arm so that **A** can easily turn his arm to the back.

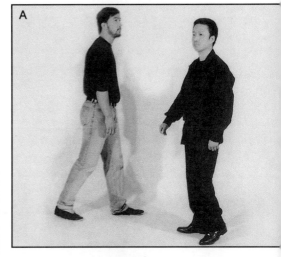

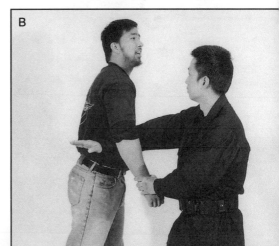

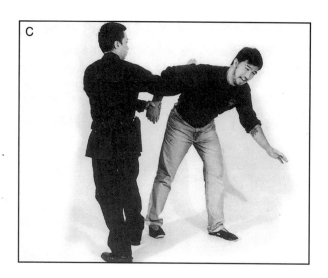

Diagram D — E:

Taking this chance, **A** immediately performs a 180° stance–turning and executes an arm-lock with a *Fook-sau* & a *Com-na-sau* (Grabbing-hand). Behind **B**'s back, **A** promptly applies a knee-strike to force **B** to kneel down.

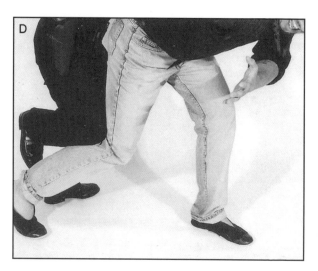

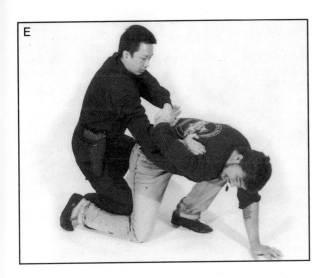

Diagram F:

With his knee on **B**'s back, **A** is now putting **B** under complete control so he can arrest him by drawing out his handcuffs.

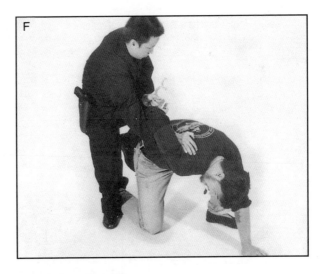

JARK-SUN BONG-SAU (側身膀手 **or** Sideling Wing-arm)

Most of the *Jark-sun Bong-sau* (Sideling Wing-arm) movements are actually organized by a Frontal Bong-sau and a turning movement.

In fact, if the attacker launches a jab, with an outward elbow, to the face or chest, the WingTsun fighter needs only execute a Thrusting-punch from underneath to strike the attacker to the face as a counter. This is the **"to counter an attack by an attack"** fighting tactic. *(See Diagram a — b: "A Punch for a punch" below)*

If the attacker executes a Thrusting-punch, with his elbow firmly pressing the arm of the WingTsun practitioner, and the pressure is too heavy for the defender to apply the above method to counter, he has to give up his own brute force and bend his arm just like a rattan cane to "unload" the pressure on it. This is the formation of *Bong-Sau*, which conforms to the motto: **"When the head is pressed down, the tail rises up".** *(Please refer to "Siu-Nim-Tau" for details).*

However, in case the pressure of the punch is too heavy and is continuously moving in that even a Frontal Bong-sau can not "unload" all the coming force, the remaining attacking force will be transferred from the Frontal Bong-sau to the upper body of the defender and turn him aside. A Sideling-stance is thus formed and the force will be totally nullified as the target disappears and the Sideling Bong-sau does not carry any force. This is the "Revolving door" principle in the WingTsun concept. *(Please refer to next page for Diagram A — B about "Revolving door")*

"A punch to a punch" (Diagram a — b)

The opponent (right) attacks a WingTsun practitioner with a jab. The defender needs only to counter with a Thrusting-punch towards the opponent to the face. Note that the WingTsun fighter is using the angles between him and his opponent to defeat the attacker when striking back.

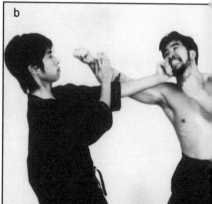

From Frontal Bong-sau to Sideling Bong-sau (Diagram A — B)

B (right) attempts to attack **A** on the chest with a Thrusting-punch. **A** contacts **B**'s punch with his left hand which is soon bent by **B**'s punching force. **A** is pushed to turn to the right side then. Since **A**'s body is turned aside, **B** loses his intended target. This is the *"Getting rid of the opponent's force"* principle of WingTsun.

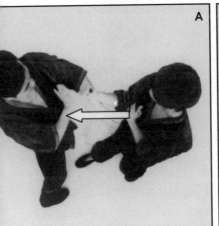

A

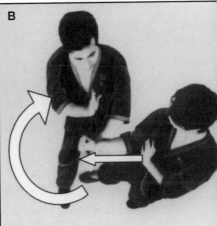

B

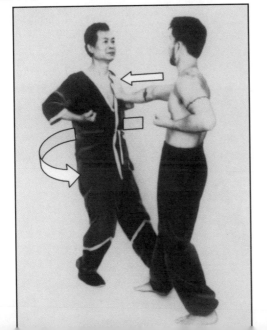

The "Revolving door" Theory:

The revolving door is not able to turn itself. It will turn to one side ONLY when another side is being pushed by the force from outside. In the left diagram, Sifu Cheung poses a frontal stance. When he is pushed by force from the left side, his upper body will turn (or better say: "**will be pushed**") to the right side.

Sideling Bong-sau in Actual Combat (Diagram 1 — 2)

B (right) tries to hit **A** on the chest with a right Thrusting-punch over the left arm of **A**. By extending out the left arm to contact **B**'s attacking arm, **A** tries to dissolve **B**'s attack. However, **B**'s powerful punch is so heavy that it creates more than adequate pressure to force **A** to change his left hand into a Bong-sau pose to unload the pressure from **B**.

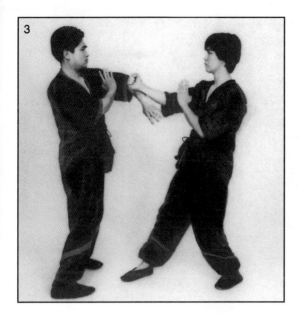

Diagram 3 — 4

By receiving the punching force, **A**'s body is pushed to turn to the right side. **B**'s attack is thus in vain.

Demonstrators:

Sifu Carson Lau
(A)

Assistant
Instructor
Lam Lap Chung
(B)

Diagram 5

A changes his right hand to a Fook-sau to control **B** on the right wrist and changes his left hand to form a Thrusting-punch ready to hit **B** on the face.

Diagram 6

While **A** is launching his left punch to **B**'s face, his right hand exerts a strong jerking force to make B fall suddenly forward. As the two forces collide with each other, **A**'s punch hence hurts **B** more severely.

COM-LAN-SAU (擒攔手 or **Grappling and Barricading-arm**) & WANG CHANG-GUEK (橫撐腳 or **Side Thrusting-kick**)

There was no Side Thrusting-kick in the Chum-Kiu set passed down by the late Great Grandmaster Yip Man. Years ago, I verified from examining some materials that there were only three basic kicking techniques in the original WingTsun system. For this reason, I finally put the Side Thrusting-kick back into the Chum-Kiu set.

There is a unique tactic in WingTsun which is that a practitioner would not kick without his arm(s) contacting the opponent. Using this tactic when the WingTsun practitioner executes a kick, the defender would find the WingTsun practitioner's

kick very difficult to defend against. The Side Thrusting-kick together with a Bar-arm can block an attack from the side yet counter a kick delivered by surprise.

If we combine the "Grappling and Barricading" technique together with a Side Thrusting-kick simultaneously, we can deal with two attackers, one to the front and one at the side, nearly all at once.

Applying a *Com-lan-sau* & a *Wang-chang-guek* to fight against two opponents in combat

Diagram A — B:

B (right) and **C** (left) attempt to attack **A** (mid) from both flanks. Under such a disadvantageous situation, **A** starts his attack in a flash. He first charges towards **B**. In this way he can at least keep a certain distance away from **C** while he is attacking **B**.

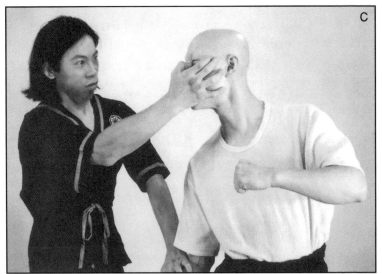

This is the *"Attack is the Best Defense"* fighting tactic in WingTsun concepts.

Demonstrators:

Sifu Ngan Tak Yee (middle)

Sifu Yan Yiu Wing (left)

Assistant instructor **Lee Wing Lok** (right)

Diagram C — D:

A applies an Eye-thrusting hand to jab the left eye of **B** with his right thumb. This is an extremely lethal movement; **B** immediately loses his fighting spirit and is in great pain. Wasting no time, **A** turns 180 to deal with **C**.

Diagram E:
While **A** is attacking **B**, **C** also attempts to attack **A**.

Diagram F — G:
A quickly lifts his right arm to fend off **C**'s punch and executes a Side thrusting-kick to counterattack **C** to his chest at once.

CHAU-CHONG-KUEN (抽撞拳 or **Lifting-punch**)

Many Wing Chun practitioners think that there is only one *"Yat-gee-chung-kuen"* or Character 'SUN' Thrusting-punch* *(or in short: Thrusting-punch)* in the fighting system. This is certainly a big mistake. *(*Please refer to "Siu-Nim-Tau" for details)*

The "Chain-punches", which are the execution of *"continuous movements by alternating Thrusting-punches"* to attack the enemy like a machine gun, is no doubt the "masterpiece" of WingTsun attack techniques. However, the Thrusting-punch CANNOT be applied for every purpose under ALL conditions. *(There is no such thing as a drug-for-all-purposes that cures any disease and, for the same reason there is no such technique that can defeat the opponent in any situation. If there were one, why should the martial artists create so many styles and so many fighting techniques?)*

In fact there are two more separate punching techniques in the barehanded sets: one in *"Chum-Kiu"* and one in *"Biu-Tze"*. They are supplementary techniques to substitute for the ineffectiveness of the "face-to-face Thrusting-punch" in certain situations.

The Lifting punch is one of the "three punching movements" in WingTsun. The way is to hit upward along a rather narrow arc-shaped route from the lower position upwards. The target being hit is either the jaw or the throat. But it can also be the face or the eye of the opponent when in certain positions. However, the lifting punch only appears once in Chum-Kiu because it is not frequently used in actual combat.

Some think that the Lifting-punch in WingTsun is the same punch as the uppercut in boxing. Actually, there are differences in exertion of force, punching direction, targets and concepts.

Uppercut in boxing

The punch is launched upward along a large oblique arc as ↖↘ from the position of the abdomen going down and then moving upwards. The upper body sways from one side to another and the head is kept low while punching. In addition, the shoulder of the punching arm moves forward along an oblique arcing route so as to increase the power of the uppercut. The punching-targets are normally to the stomach, the waist or the lower jaw of the opponent.

Lifting-punch in WingTsun:

Based on the elbow force first, the fist is lifted up with a small oblique arc as ↖↘ , which is almost along a vertical punching route in the last trail of the punch. The Lifting-punch is so-called because most of the punching force comes from the "sudden up-lifting power of the upper body," especially when the fist comes closer to its target. As the lifting-punch normally focuses on the most fragile parts of the body such as the lower jaw, throat or sometimes the face and eye of the opponent, it is much easier to knock out the victim with a single punch.

LIFTING-PUNCH IN WINGTSUN:
Mainly lifting the upper body upward with the punch along a narrow arcing route forms the force of the lifting punch.

UPPERCUT IN BOXING: The punch is executed along a big arcing route.

A

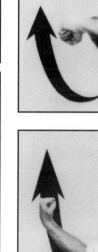

1

2

B

3

Two examples for the applications of Lifting-punch
Under different situations

Left: An opponent is powerfully grasping the waist of the WingTsun fighter (right) and his head is sticking to the chest of the WingTsun fighter so closely and tightly that it is totally impossible for him to counter the opponent with face-to-face Straight-line Thrusting-punches to the face. Under this situation, the WingTsun fighter would press down on the back of the neck of his opponent with one hand and, at the same time, apply a Lifting-punch to hit the opponent in the face.

Right: When a WingTsun fighter is clasped by his opponent with both arms on the neck trying to attack him with a knee-strike and the elbows of the attacker block the way of the straight-line Thrusting-punches, the WingTsun fighter, not to be attacked by the knee-strike, immediately blocks the knee with a slapping palm (Gum-sau) and, simultaneously, applies a Lifting-punch with the other hand to hit the opponent to the lower jaw.

Lifting-punch in Actual Combat: (Diagram a — b)

A (right) is confronting **B**. When **A** tries to attack **B** by rushing forward and launching a Thrusting-punch to the face, **B** immediately lowers his body to dodge the attack. **A**'s punch is therefore in vain and he is very close to **B** at the same moment.

Changing to a continuous movement with the same hand
——— A unique fighting concept in the WingTsun System

For most kungfu styles, if the attacker fails to hit his opponent with the first punch *(this is so-called "the attacking movement turns old" in Chinese kungfu terminology")*, normally he has to draw back the first punch before he applies the second punch to attack with another hand. However, under this situation, a skilful WingTsun practitioner needs not draw back the "old punch" and then apply another punch with another hand. He only needs to continue his attack by changing to another movement with the same hand without drawing it back first.

(Diagram c — d)

Therefore, **A** only needs to change the missed punch into a *Gum-sau* (Pinning-hand) movement from the outside to press the back of the neck of the opponent. Nearly at the same time, **A** applies the left Lifting-punch to hit the face of **B**.

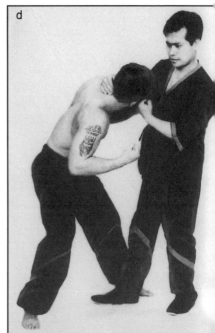

CHING-SUN-GUEK (正身腳 or **Frontal Thrusting-kick**) & NOI-MOON FOOK-SAU (內門伏手 or **Indoor-area Bridge-on arm**)

The Frontal Thrusting-kick is a very common kicking technique in WingTsun. This movement is, though practiced with both fists kept under the armpits in the Chum-Kiu set, actually so flexible that we can work it out with any suitable hand technique when applying it in actual combat.

As WingTsun practitioners, we normally like to apply primarily hand techniques to attack and defend in actual combats. This is because we can use "two arms" for fighting but we can only apply "one leg" to attack or defend at a time since we always need another leg to stand on the ground.

However, this preference dose not mean that we have weak kicking techniques but rather the reason is, we never abuse the application of the kicks.

According to WingTsun theory, if one lays emphasis on attacking and defending with legs unnecessarily when his hands can deal with the same situations or even better, it would be absolutely unwise because it is quite easy for the kicker to "lose his balance" that can create an advantageous opportunity for his opponent to defeat him.

The Frontal Thrusting-kick (正身腳), when associated with the Double

Noi-Moon Fook-sau (雙內門伏手), is a *"countering an attack by an attack"* (以打為消) technique, which can attack the opponent by surprise and restrain the opponent's withdrawal by the grappling both of his hands.

Diagram 1:

B suddenly grasps **A** by the wrists with both hands. **A** knows that he cannot break loose of the control by **B** easily due to **B**'s powerful two-handed grip.

101

Diagram 2 — 3:

Referring to the motto *"Refrain from fighting against the fully defended part of your opponent but attack his unprepared part"* (棄實擊虛), **A** directly applies a Frontal Thrusting-kick to attack **B** on the abdomen and, at the same time, turns up both palms to counter-control **B**'s wrists with the Double Indoor-area Fook-sau movement.

Diagram 4 — 5:

With both hands grappled by **A**, **B** cannot even withdraw a step when he is being kicked by **A**. Wasting no time, **A** continues his next attack by taking a step forward, changing his right hand into a Slapping-hand to trap both arms of **B**, and applies the left Thrusting-punch to hit **B** on his face.

FROM DAI-BONG-SAU (低膀手 or **Lower Wing-arms**)
TO
MAN-SAU (問手 or **Inquisitive-arms**)

In the Chum-Kiu set, the Lower *Bong-Sau* (Wing-arms) and *Man-Sau* (Inquisitive-arms) are "Double-movements*". The same movements are practiced by both hands in the sets, but are only applied in actual combat by a single hand individually or associated with other techniques — just like assembling two differently functioning tools together to form another tool especially adapted to deal with different tasks under particular conditions. *(* For "Double-movements" please refer to the book "Wing Tsun Kuen" for details.)*

There is consistency in the change from lower Bong-sau to Man-sau. The force of WingTsun is flexible and elastic so all the movements applied possess the force like that of the spring or a rattan cane. And this force will be "retracted" under great pressure. *(Note: "Retract" means: A rattan cane or a spring would not retract by itself.* **They are "forced" to retract or bend <u>ONLY</u> by external force** *and their elasticity can always be restored.)*

Once the outer pressure is reduced, the force of the rattan cane or the spring rebounds.

The "faster" the outer pressure fades away, the "quicker" the rebounded force will be formed. The more powerful the outer pressure appears, the more powerful the rebound force will be. This is the motto of ***"stay with it when it comes, follow right after it when it withdraws. If your arm is freed, just thrust it outwards"*** (來留去送、甩手直衝).

The "force-unloading" (卸力 or *"Se-Lik"* in WingTsun terms) feature of the rattan cane or the spring should also be noted. Something like rattan cane or the spring bends with heavy pressure at one end. When the bending state reaches a certain limitation, the objects exerting pressure will be "unloaded" and slide downward due to the drooping angle of one end of the cane or the spring. Once the pressure disappears suddenly, the cane or the spring would rebound right away.

The rebound-force becomes proportional to the previous pressure — *"The greater the pressure, the stronger the resistance"* — this is the characteristic of "elasticity" of the cane and the spring.

The change from lower Bong-sau to Man-sau consists of the same feature as above. And it also accords with the principle of "flexibility" in WingTsun fighting concepts.

Illustrations on *"Stay with it when it comes, follow right after it when it withdraws. If your arm is freed, just thrust it outwards"*

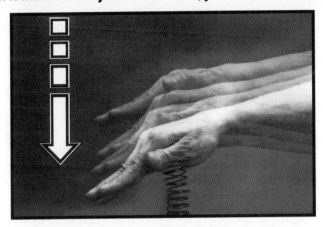

Diagram 1: The force of WingTsun has the same nature as that of a spring. When the outer pressure is applied downwards, the spring is being retracted but its resistance depends on the outer force: *"greater the pressure, stronger the resistance"*. Once the force retreats, it will reinstate right away.

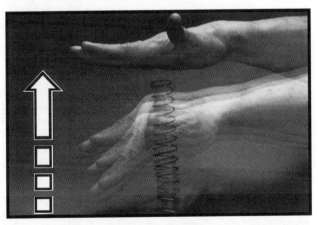

Diagram 2: If the pressure disappears suddenly, the spring will rebound right away. The rebound-force is proportional to the pressure withdrawn. That is: *the quicker the pressure disappears, the greater speed the spring bounces back with.*

Character of the rattan cane:

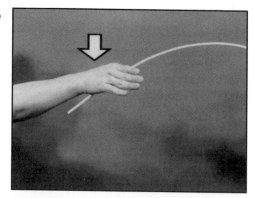

Diagram 1:
When a rattan cane (or a spring) is being pressed at one end, it bends according to the downward force.

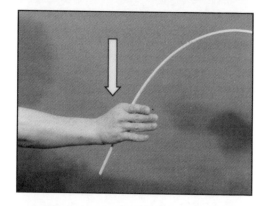

Diagram 2:
The stronger the pressure, the bigger the bending state that will be formed. This turns the rattan cane into a curve shape.

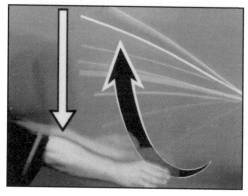

Diagram 3:
When the cane is being pressed to droop down close to a vertical angle, the pressure thus loses support of the cane and slips down suddenly. At the same moment, the cane rebounds upwards with a powerful snap due to the force provided from the previous pressure.

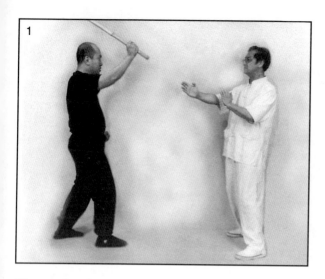

Diagram 1 — 3:

A (right) confronts **B** who is holding a cane. **B** attempts to attack **A** with a head-on downward smash with the cane. **A**, instead of making a step backwards, dashes forward and extends his right arm out to the forward-upward direction to form a Man-sau movement.

Diagram 4 — 6:
The cane slides down along the oblique angle of **A**'s Man-sau; **B**'s attack is thus in vain. Right after deflecting the downward attacking cane to one side, **A** immediately sinks down his arm and changes it into a Jut-sau to suppress the cane. Taking this chance **A** launches a Frontal palm, striking to the ear of **B**.

Demonstrators:

Grandmaster Leung Ting (right)   **Sifu Lam Wing Fai** (left)

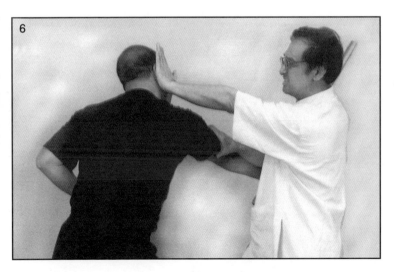

DAI-BONG-SAU Vs SPINNING-KICK

The spinning kicks (as in Taekwondo for example) and roundhouse kicks (as in Thai boxing for example) both belong to the high kicks of those styles. However, they are two different leg techniques in presentation.

The roundhouse-kick can be dissolved by applying *Shang-Ha Gaun-sau** (上下捭手 or "High and Low Splitting-blocks"), *Gwat-sau** (刮手 or "Wiping-arm") or Ko *Tan-sau** (高攤手 or "High Palm-up arm"). *(*Please refer to "Siu-Nim-Tau" and "Biu-Tze" for details)* The spinning kick is based on the force of the leg coordinating with the momentum of the spinning-body. Therefore it is quite inefficient if we apply those techniques like a Gwat-sau or High Tan-sau to dissolve it similar to what we do to dissolve the roundhouse kick. The reason is that even if we can block the upper leg, we cannot block the "hooking-in" lower leg, which would be like blocking the lower part of a nunchaku or a three-section-cudgel. However, if we know another usage of the Lower Bong-sau, we can effectively dissolve the spinning-kick by applying the fighting tactic *"to counter an attack by an attack."*

The *Dai Bong-sau* in Chum-Kiu is also called *Noi Bong-sau* (內膀手 or "Internal Wing-arm") by people of some Wing Chun branches, and is the opposite of the function of the ordinary *Bong-sau*, yet closer to that of *Kau-sau* (摣手 or "Circling-block").

Left: The application of Gwat-sau to dissolve roundhouse-kick is effective.

Right: However, if one applies the Gwat-sau to dissolve a spinning-kick, even though he can block the thigh of the kicker, the hooking-in lower leg would still kick him.

Diagram 1 — 2:

B attempts to attack **A** with a spinning-kick. **A**, instead of stepping backwards, darts forward and changes one arm into the Lower Bong-sau, with a Sideward palm as a protective palm.

111

Diagram 3:

The Lower Bong-sau forms an outward triangle, which is good enough for keeping the bending lower leg of the kicker from hooking in.

Diagram 4:

Meanwhile, **A** charges in with an extremely powerful step to crush **B** on his standing leg, with the lower Bong-sau swinging upwards to form a Man-sau movement. This action makes **B** lose his balance and he is flung several feet away.

Demonstrators:
    Grandmaster Leung Ting   **Sifu Christopher Collins**

112

CHE-CHANG-GUEK (斜撑脚 or **Slant Thrusting-kick**)

The *Che-chang-guek* or Slant Thrusting-kick, alias *Che-gwa-guek* (斜掛脚 or "Slant Hanging-kick"), consists of only one turning kick to the left in the Chum-Kiu set and is especially applied to deal with the opponent standing behind.

The significance of the turning kick lies in the 180° turning of the body while the left leg alone is kicking in a slant side-wards direction.

Besides the 180° turning and kicking, we can deal with the opponent standing sideways in a special situation by turning to a smaller angle flexibly. *(Please refer to: "Why is there no Slant Thrusting-kick to the right side in Chum-Kiu?" of "Concept and Theories")*

Diagram A — C:
The late Great Grandmaster Yip Man demonstrating the sequence from the Slant Thrusting-kick to Side Pinning-hand. Note that after fully extending the leg, Yip steps with his left foot to where it reaches.

113

Diagram 1 — 2:

A (Mid) is confronting **B** (left); while **C** (right) is standing behind him a bit farther away, awaiting a better chance to start an attack. While **A** is dealing with **B**, **C** suddenly steps forward and attempts to make a foray by punching **A** from behind.

Demonstrators:

Sifu Carson Lau (mid)

Assistant Instructor **Lam Lap Chung** (left)

Assistant Instructor **Wong Wai Leung** (right)

Diagram 3 — 4:
Seeing **C**'s contemplation, **A** suddenly turns to **C** and launches a Slant Thrusting-kick at his abdomen. In the mean time, he applies a grappling hand to pull **B** downward-sideward so **B** cannot attack him while he is dealing with **C**.

Diagram 5 — 6:
C never expects that **A** is so alert and, while dealing with **B**, can still be quick enough to attack him by surprise with the heavy turning kick. He cannot avoid being hurt seriously and falls several feet away. **A** seizes the chance to continue counterattacking **B**.

JARK-SUN GUM-SAU (側身撳手 or **Sideling Pinning-hand**)

There are not many techniques that deal with lower-level attacks in the WingTsun system; especially there are no "crouching" movements dealing with those so-called very low attacks. Due to the ingenious construction of the unique WingTsun stance cooperating with magnetic-like footwork with the *"close-range pursuing attack"** (貼身短打) fighting tactic, a WingTsun fighter can easily jam the stance of the opponent making it difficult for him to apply any kick to attack the lower part of the body.

In particular, when a WingTsun fighter executes the *"Violent attacks with Breaching steps"** (迫步密襲) fighting tactic that gives the opponent no chance to even stand stably, in this situation, it would be impossible for him to apply any kick. This is the motto of *"hitting the head, no kick"** (打頭無腳). *(* Please refer to the book "WingTsun Mottos and Concepts" for details)*

This was the main reason that traditional grandmasters such as the late Great Grandmaster Yip Man or others regarded fighting techniques associated with the lower part of the body as "top secrets" and did not show their ordinary students these techniques. *(This is also the "secret" for my headstudents and for me to teach a lot of champions of other martial arts who are already experts in kicking!)*

However, it is still a possibility for a WingTsun practitioner to be attacked by the mid-and-lower-level kicks in a confrontation with an opponent. For this reason, there are three movements in WingTsun to dissolve the kicks: they are *Gaun-sau*, *Gwat-sau* and *Gum-sau*. Generally, Gwat-sau is applied to deal with the roundhouse kick. Gaun-sau and Sideling Gum-sau can be used to deal with side-kicks, frontal kicks, snap-kicks and so on. Different techniques depend on different angles and positions between the WT practitioner and his opponent in a confrontation.

Lower: If the front-arm of a WT fighter is placed at the indoor-area of the front leg of the opponent in pre-fighting positions, he can directly apply a Gwat-sau or a Gaun-sau to deal with the kick.

Upper: If the WingTsun fighter places his front arm at the outdoor-area of the front leg of the opponent in the pre-fighting position, he can launch a Gaun-sau to dissolve the kick. (*About terms of "Indoor-area" and "Outdoor-area", please refer to the book "Siu-Nim-Tau" for details)

Lower: When the opponent kicks, if the WingTsun fighter's front arm is at the indoor-area, it would be too slow for him to apply a Gaun-sau as he has to make a big circle to the outdoor-area. Hence the quickest way is to apply a Sideling Gum-sau.

CONCEPTS AND THEORIES

FRONTAL STANCE, SIDE-LEANING STANCE & ADVANCING STANCE

The stance and footwork are very important in Chum-Kiu techniques training.

The *Yee-Gee-Kim-Yeung-Ma* (二字拑羊馬), or literately translated as the *"Character 'TWO' Adduction Stance"*, implies that both soles should make a 60° angle in the stance *(so the whole Frontal-stance is an "equilateral triangle")*. The position of both toes and heels thus forms a shape like the Chinese character " 二 ".

However, according to the late Great Grandmaster Yip Man, all the Wing Tsun stances are called "Character 'TWO' Adduction Stance" regardless of frontal stance, side-leaning stance *(or "Sideling-stance" in short)*, or advancing stance.

The only difference is that the character " 二 " for the frontal stance is in standard writing yet the character *"//"* in the Sideling-stance and the Advancing-stance *(alias Chunk-chi-ma 衝刺馬 or "Storming-stance")* is in italic style. *(Please see the white lines in the following two photos)*

The center of gravity should be in the middle of a Frontal-stance. While posing a Sideling-stance or Advancing-stance, the body weight should be entirely laid on the rear leg yet the front leg is strong enough to draw the rear leg forwards.

When changing a Frontal-stance to another stance, the upper body should not swing while turning the legs. In another word, the center of gravity has to be very stable during moving.

The distance between both feet should always be the same despite posing any stance. This is the only way to maintain the body balance. *(Please refer to "Dynamic Wing Tsun Kungfu" for stances for details)*.

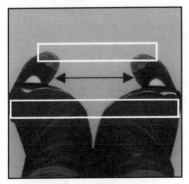 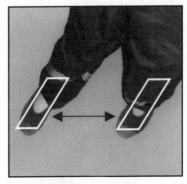

Left: The Frontal stance   **Right: The Sideling stance**

Mistakes A & B: The stance is too wide. When turning to a sideling stance, the body weight cannot totally shift to the rear leg. Therefore, when an enemy attacks, he cannot move his upper body completely away thus removing the target. *(Note 1)*

Mistakes 1 & 2: The stance is too narrow and too low. Posing a stance like this would make it difficult to move swiftly and make turning a clumsy process. *(Note 2)*

Mistakes a & b: This is a very common error for most of the Wing Chun people. Due to the lack of linking force between the knees, the legs of the advancing stance become changed to a "T-shape" relative to each other. In such a stance, it would be easy for the attacker to attack him with snap-kick to the groin when stepping forward. *(Note 3)*

Note 1: When turning the Frontal-stance to a Sideling-stance, the weight of the upper body should be totally shifted onto the rear leg. This is the only way we can "delete" the target <u>completely</u> from the original location our enemy wishes to attack. Once there is "no target," the attack will be in vain. Looking at the stance of the defender in diagrams A & B, part of the defender's body-weight is still on the front leg. In this case, the practitioner is not able to "totally" remove his upper-body (the target) from the center to one side. The opponent can still hit him easily.

Note 2: There is a saying <u>"Difficult to keep the body balanced by a high stance yet difficult to move by a low stance"</u> in kungfu theories. Some Wing Chun people borrow the idea from other kungfu styles to believe that "a lower stance is more stable". Thus, they violate the taboo of "Difficult to move by lower stance". The truth is: although the WingTsun stance is high, we do have a unique way and footwork to resolve the above problem by means of the "adduction-force". That is why we can move quickly yet stably.

Note 3: Please refer to the book "WingTsun Mottos and Concepts"; or the text **"Theory on Footwork"** in the book and tape of **"Dynamic Wing Tsun Kungfu"** for details.

121

WHY SHOULD WE *"BEWARE WHEN APPLYING AN INDOOR-AREA SLAPPING-HAND MOVEMENT"*?

There is a saying *"Beware when applying an Indoor-area Slapping-hand Movement"* (拍手忌內門) according to WingTsun (Wing Chun) fighting theories. Many WingTsun (Wing Chun) practitioners have heard this motto but don't really understand the reasons behind it. Therefore, some of them have the idea that they must not apply any indoor area Slapping-hand!

The so-called *"Beware when applying an Indoor-area Slapping-hand Movement"* motto is only a special warning to the WingTsun (Wing Chun) practitioners by our more experienced experts of the older generations. It does not mean that we can "never" apply the Indoor-area Slapping-hand or we would have said that *"it is wrong to apply any Indoor-area Slapping-hand"* instead.

In fact, *"Beware when applying an Indoor-area Slapping-hand Movement"* means we must be highly alert in the <u>"coordination of the attacking and controlling movements taken together"</u> during the moment we are using a *Pak-sau* (Slapping-hand) to slap down the front arm of our opponent from the Indoor-area. Otherwise, we will be attacked before we attack.

The biggest difference between the WingTsun system and other kungfu styles is that we often apply the mottos like *"**Defend and Attack Simultaneously**"* (消打同時) and *"**Give attention to both hands simultaneously**"* (兩手兼顧). That is to say, we seldom slap away the hand of the opponent and "then" launch a counterattack. Thus this concept is very different from the tactics of *"Dissolve the attacking movement <u>first</u> and <u>then</u> counter"* (先消後打) or *"Dissolve an attack with one arm and then counterattack with the same arm"* (連消帶打) as in most of the other martial arts. *(Although the second tactic is a bit better than the first one, it, however, still takes <u>two movements</u> that occupy <u>two different timed sequences</u> to "dissolve and counter".)*

As in Diagram A — C: If we do not attack our opponent with one hand while applying a Slapping-hand to slap the hand of the opponent from the indoor-area, we may create an excellent chance for our opponent to attack us at almost the same time.

Therefore, we must pay attention **not just** to the **"coordination of both hands simultaneously"** but **"coordination of footwork while the upper limbs are attacking and defending"** (手腿合一) **at the same time**, especially under a condition as mentioned above. *(Diagram 1 — 3)*

To sum up, the difference in the WingTsun mottos from that of other martial arts is in the controlling of the timing of the techniques.

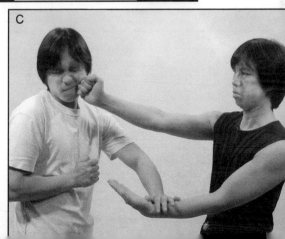

Diagram A — C:

A (left) attempts to attack **B**. He uses the left hand to press down **B**'s front arm but he does not launch the right hand to attack **B** <u>at the same time</u>. The result is that **A** offers **B** the best chance to attack him first.

Diagram 1 — 3:

In attempting to attack **B**, **A** uses both his hands to apply a *Pak-sau* and a Thrusting-punch at the same time when moving in.

Moreover, **A** dashes forward to apply the *"Close-range-pursuing-attack"* (貼身短打) tactic which totally controls **B** by trapping both of his arms while punching.

THE CORRECT AND INCORRECT WAY OF CHANGING THE FRONTAL BONG-SAU INTO A SIDELING BONG-SAU

On practicing Chum-Kiu, there are some people emphasize too much on the angle of the Sideling-stance when turning a Frontal Bong-sau to a Sideling-stance. Some people even try to turn their upper body to form an excessive 90° angle!

Disproportionate turning is not advisable in the Sideling-stance. The reason one turns a Frontal Bong-sau into a Sideling Bong-sau is because he is supposed to have received the coming force from the attacker with the Wing-arm but the force is too strong and made him turn aside. In fact, the opponent is still standing "in front of him." *(Please refer to pg. 89 to 91 for detailed explanation.)*

Indeed, 45° angle turning would be more than adequate for a WingTsun practitioner to shift all the body weight onto the rear leg so he can totally remove the "target" away from center and to the flank. This makes the attack of the opponent in vain. Once the Sideling Bong-sau unloads the oncoming force, one should turn back to the frontal pose to counterattack without delay.

If the angle of the stance is too big, he will spend too much time in turning back when applying a counter. *"The longer the distance, the longer the time one needs to travel from one end to another end";* this is the definition in WingTsun concepts.

A: CORRECT SIDELING BONG-SAU
A 45° angle is enough for the Sideling-stance to totally diminish the coming force of the attacker.

B: INCORRECT SIDELING BONG-SAU
Turning the upper body in a bigger angle than necessary can waste more time when launching a counter attack.

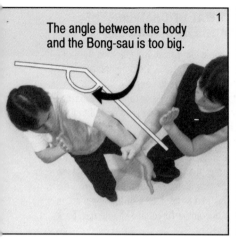

1 The angle between the body and the Bong-sau is too big.

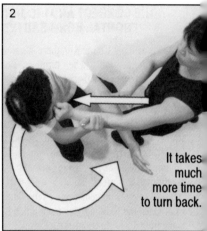

2 It takes much more time to turn back.

Diagram 1 — 2: The bigger the turning angle of the Sideling Bog-sau, the longer the distance is for a WingTsun practitioner to counter. That is to say, it takes much more time to launch a punch and he may offer his opponent an excellent chance to execute the second attack.

Diagram A — B: The smaller the turning angle of the Sideling Bong-sau, the shorter distance is for a WingTsun practitioner to turn back to the Frontal stance. That is to say, it takes a short time to fight back.

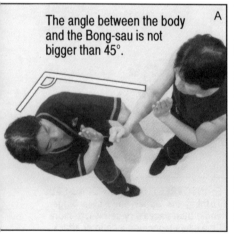

A The angle between the body and the Bong-sau is not bigger than 45°.

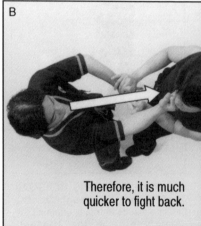

B Therefore, it is much quicker to fight back.

126

HOW TO DEAL WITH THE OPPONENT SKILFUL IN KICKING?

Many WingTsun practitioners prefer to keep a certain distance away from an opponent who is skilful in kicking so as to avoid being hurt by the strong leg-techniques. Actually, this is an incorrect decision that offers their opponent more opportunity to defeat them.

If you keep a certain distance away from your opponent in a confrontation for such a reason, it would be like a saying, *"using your weak point to fight against the strong point of your enemy"*. The reason is simple: because the arm is shorter than the leg, if both fighters attack each other at the same time at long-range, before your fist can touch your opponent, you are already hurt by the kicker.

Do consult any skilful kickers and you will find out the truth. What they are afraid of is to face an opponent who is standing too close or even clutching them in combat. Under such conditions the kicker would find it very difficult to launch a kick.

However, it is just the opposite for the WingTsun fighters. As we are "experts" in dealing with opponents at close-range, we can gain more advantages in such situations than our opponent. The *"close-range pursuing-attacks" are the* tactics specifically used to deal with opponents with skilful kicking techniques or those who are taller. These tactics are also applied because a taller person normally has longer arms and longer legs. However, their advantages become disadvantages if they are fighting with a WingTsun practitioner at a very close range.

The motto *"Violent continuous attacks with Breaching steps"* applied with chain-punches and nonstop steps are the best fighting tactic to defeat a skilful kicker before he can apply any leg-technique to attack. This is also the concept of *"hitting the head, no kick"* as was stated on *pg. 117 "Sideling Gum-Sau".*

WRONG TACTICS TO DEAL WITH A SKILFUL KICKER

DIAGRAM A — D:

Keeping a long distance away from the opponent who is skilful at kicking, blindly dodging aside, or retreating with big steps while the attacker is executing a kick will only create more chances for the opponent to launch continuous attacks with kicks.

A

As in these diagrams, when **B** (right) attempts to get away from **A** while he is attacking with a spinning kick, **B** does not know that to step backward he actually creates another chance for **A** to launch the second leg-attack at a rather long-range.

The motto of "Hitting the head, no kick!"

Diagram 1 — 2:

A (right) stands close to face **B**, though he knows **B** is good at kicking. When **B** applies a roundhouse kick, **A seizes** the chance to dash into the stance of **B** with *"Breaching steps"*. **A** applies the left Gaun-sau to block the right kick of **B** and at the same time, applies a right Thrusting-punch to counterattack **B** to the face. The "Breaching steps" soon crash **B**'s stance to make him lose his balance and he has absolutely no chance to launch the next kick before he falls down.

WHY IS THERE NO SLANT THRUSTING-KICK
TO THE RIGHT SIDE IN CHUM-KIU?

It seems very strange to many Wing Chun people that there is no slant thrusting-kick to the right side in the Chum-Kiu set. As a result, some Wing Chun practitioners have added in a Right Slant Thrusting-kick after the kick to the left side so as to make up for the "missing kick" in their mind. *(However, have those people ever thought deeply as to why it is that our great grandmasters, who were wise enough to found the whole system and all the barehanded sets, could forget this "missing slant-kick to the right side"? Why should they all need us, after so many hundreds of years, to correct this "mistake" in these modern times?)*

Actually, the reasons for only the Left Slant thrusting-kick in Chum Kiu are as follows:

Firstly, our founder designed the sets so that the place that we start performing the sets is the same place where we finish the whole set. This is how all the sets work and it does not matter if it is the weapon sets or the barehanded ones.

There is no exception in the Chum-Kiu set. Hence, after we kick with the left foot with a Slant Thrusting-kick to the left side, we drag our body back to the original place where we start practicing the set.

Unlike the sets of the other styles, all the kungfu sets in WingTsun (Wing Chun) require very little space for practice. It is because we have to learn how to fight even in narrow spaces where the other martial arts are not able to fully apply their wide-ranging movements. There is a saying: *"to practice the whole set within the range for a cow to lie on"*. (拳打臥牛之地) The purpose of *"To start and close the set at the same place"* is to educate the practitioners to control the correct position of the footwork.

However, the most important reason behind this idea is that the Slant Thrusting-kick is a "sneaky technique" designed to attack the opponent by surprise. As with *Hau Gum-sau* (後撳手 or "Backward Pinning-hand") in the Siu-Nim-Tau set, it is rarely applied in normal circumstances.

If people are normally good at using the right arm and the right leg to attack and defend and then we practice this movement with both legs, most of the practitioners will automatically apply the right foot in urgent situations due to their natural habits. Therefore, our founder does not teach us the right Slant Thrusting-kick to "force" us to practice the left leg (normally the weaker leg) only.

On the other hand, most of the people emphasize defending attacks made by the right hand or the right foot. Considering this, if the WingTsun practitioner can apply a Thrusting-kick to the left side skillfully which is actually "abnormal" to most people, this would certainly make this technique a "surprise attack."

This is the main reason we have only one Slant Thrusting-kick to the left side in Chum-Kiu.